the body wars

pitt poetry series

ed ochester, editor

the body wars

jan beatty

university of pittsburgh press

Published by the University of Pittsburgh Press, Pittsburgh, Pa., 15260

Copyright © 2020, Jan Beatty

Printed on acid-free paper

10 9 8 7 6 5 4 3 2 1

ISBN 13: 978-0-8229-6624-1

ISBN 10: 0-8229-6624-7

Cover art: *insidemymind*, Michael Lotenero, www.lotenero.com

Cover design: Joel W. Coggins

CONTENTS

the body wars

1

And now the dark air is like fire on my skin
And even the moonlight is blinding

Townes Van Zandt, "Rake," *Delta Momma Blues*

The Body Wars

I walked into the woods bleeding, I
left the town and mourned.
Midnight in Alaska, still light and I
was alone, walking into the Sitka woods,
it had been 1 year since I'd bled, and
longer since I'd fucked anyone, I
was propelled forward, into the thickness,
into the needles and dirt of Sitka spruce
and stupidly not even afraid of bear.
My father, the person I clung to, needed
to stay alive, had died six months before.
He was the only one who made sense in my body,
and his leaving was the impossible thing.
I didn't yet know my own wars and how to name them.
So during my father's sickness,
when I stopped bleeding, the gynecologist said,
well, it's stress, and did I
know that in World War II, the women
paratroopers stopped having periods?
I was stunned by his directness, intensity, earnestness.
You are in a war, he said.
I didn't know what to do with that.
And so I got on a boat to Alaska, the
Alaska Marine Highway, slept on the deck
until I froze, then the shipmen gave me
a hanging bunk and slipped me
food from the cafeteria. They said, You can
sleep here, but watch out for the bow-thrusters.
I had no idea what they meant, until the sound
burst open and my berth swayed—and
it was time to get off. It was a time of great
changes, and days later I'm wandering
the woods at midnight, feeling lost and found

in this Northern place, and it was there
I felt the blood start to move, felt a rising and
falling and the stream down my leg—and I cried in
the forest alone, for my beautiful father, gone
too soon, for myself and all my ignorance:
not even knowing my own wars—
the ones already fought,
or the many to still come.

2

The struggle has always been inner, and is played out
in outer terrains.

Gloria Anzaldúa

Stormday

It never occurred to me until this stormday, while swinging in the wind, that trees are travelers, in the ordinary sense.

John Muir

I'm in the desert reading about the Sierra Nevada forests,
thinking of storms. My astrologer said it wasn't
my job—but the three colliding transits making me
crazy.

All these daily lightning strikes are wearing me down,
and when I read John Muir I ask, *Am I waving or bending?*
He talks about the madroños with "red bark and large
glass leaves" —and I become smaller and made full
at the same time.

What would it be like to be stormless?

It wouldn't be life, and the "sea waves on a shelving shore"
would sink into flatness. Truly, it's the floating, dropping
in so deep that I love.

Like when Muir *enters* the song, the trees singing, and
talks about the "annihilation of years."
What could be better?

He says: ". . . I suddenly recognized a sea-breeze, as it came
sifting through the palmettos and blooming vine-tangles,
which at once awakened and set free a thousand dormant
associations . . ."

Where were they—those thousand?

The air full/the instant of opening/
the leap immediate—

Those thousand, romantic moments of a life/
and he said that now he was a boy/that now/
". . . all the intervening years had been annihilated . . ."

Beautiful minute, oh minute of gone years.

Crushing It

Halloween, the pizza delivery girl said:
Are you dressed like a trucker?
No, I said, *I'm supposed to be*
a Western woman writer.
Oh, she said, *I like it.*
Someone else thought I was Eddie Vedder,
someone else, Tommy Morello from
Rage Against the Machine.
Maybe it was the ballcap flannel vibe, but
I was shooting for Pam Houston, dreaming
of Wyoming and the Big Horns.
Like when the cab driver in Dublin
said, *You look exactly like Anastacia,*
she's a singer, she's beautiful—
except she has long blonde hair.
Then I crossed the road and the guy
at airport security said, *This way, sir.*
Once at the make-up counter in Macy's,
I asked for some skin cream.
The skin specialist stood a foot from
my face and said, *I'm sorry, sir,*
we don't carry that line.
Pam Houston, where are you now?
I know you like cowboys but
the Big Horns call me daily—it's wide
open that I need, where the big road snakes
and cattle move so slowly, they won't even call me
ma'am, sir, or Neil Young.
I'm here, in Pittsburgh,
crushing on you.

Gunlover

But what you've done here
Is put yourself between a bullet and a target
And it won't be long before
You're pulling yourself away

Citizen Cope

I love the long barrel, the extension.
The shape, the round, and the sharp of it,
spinning chamber and clicking sounds—
the shine when it's polished,
and the beautiful dense heavy in my hand.
Like it's something that means something—
and I know that's not something to say,
because I don't want anyone to die,
because trajectory, because 1 in the chamber,
7 in the clip, because tracer bullet, trace it back to
I can't own a gun, curved handle—

It's like the slamming down a vertical street, all
the while, the language I thought I had for it
narrowing and falling, and the blue/green flowers
on the cover of my Buddhist book
break fluid like a guitar solo,
and I love the slide of it,
the slamming repetition until the break————
cracks fluid,
until the pop——
the wilding————
there's a cannonball inside me waiting to
sling—first shot and all the shots

and the hills split,
I'm so tired with the walking in to them.
Don't lose my stride into that other
world,

and there's a truck with high tin sides in my mind,
and everything now is flesh-colored, and walking
away, and walking away, so
no, I can't own a gun—
so no, loading it up and feeling that metal,
I would use it, I
would split open one day/
I would shoot it—

and the silver barrel, the round and sharp aren't
the thing—it's the hammer down,
and I'm the bullet —and I'm the target,
shell of a person, sleeping charlatan—
and that break inside me,
explosion of the con artist inside me—
sometimes I want to make a deal with beauty
no matter what.

Drunken Trees

Because permafrost melts, it causes
a lot of erosion. A lot of trees can't stand up
straight. If the erosion gets worse,
everything goes with it.

              Sarah James, Native American Elder

The trees are drinking again, bending and ready
to fall.
It's not just the trees.
Nothing can grow straight—the ground is
shifting—the spinning of it rocks me,
the off-kilter/
what is moving and what is steady?
Five planets retrograde and dirt doesn't
seem like dirt anymore—
If the rivers change course, does it mean
that my heart can change direction?
Will our feelings rush and flood into
the bodies of others?
The bending, leaning humans are littering
the sidewalks of every city, and
I'm afraid of what happens next:
will our hearts break open and
forget to be hearts?
Will our sturdy legs buckle into chairs
that others sit on? Will we wish
for everything horizontal until
the earth is finally flat into the sea?
Jesus still shows up in cheap tin mirrors
all over New Mexico Taos, and he's
not moving yet—the virgin mary might
finally speak up and say that virginity crap
was an inside job—she was paid off,
and really Frida Kahlo was the son of god—

her love of the body and masturbation
kept things moving, shifting—and the
only thing paramount was pleasure—
oh trees   please stand up
We are sorry—dear trees that speak for
the wobbly lives we lead—bending,
leaning into the expanse, the vast
circumference of now,
the circle of the circle of the
globe—
we love you,
orb of our sphere,
continental shelf of our move and shift—
as we crack into the mad ocean.

On the Anniversary of Charlottesville

Cooler today, 81 degrees.
There's a storm moving through Alamogordo &
Ruidoso. What beautiful swirling in these
names: Lupe, Obadiah, Slade.
Radio says a tornado hit Eagle Nest,
north of Taos. Ski country. Hasn't happened
in 10 years.

Spike Lee's being interviewed wearing a "Thank God
for Bob Mueller" teeshirt, while fire tornadoes
slam the West & arsonists are burning people's lives.
NFL players kneeling & raising their fists (thank god)
on this first anniversary of Charlottesville.
State of emergency declared in Virginia please
don't let anything happen.
It's National Lion Day & the sun will be bloodied
tomorrow. The moon in Leo & how
did we thrash back to the '60s race wars or
we never left. Moon opposes Mars|squares Uranus|

Solar eclipse in these mountains—headaches
for days. I can feel the changes.
Spike Lee's *BlacKKKlansman* releases today,
he said until the U.S. owns that it was founded on genocide
& slavery—we'll never get better & the world's
in a fire tornado on Highway 60, up from Angel Fire.
Deranged air, high winds, flash floods, hail yesterday
in the I-25 corridor.

In Cibola County, storms moving towards Roswell
on its way out of the Milky Way &
even the alien heads on fire.

Double-Cut

I was double-cut:
once in the womb with a hanger,
once when I came out.

In the asylum, the hanging
bulb of the playground kingdom
birthed the hunger in me—

children staring in cast-off tees
the paint-chipped metal carousel
with struck-stupid infants strapped
                                    in

The golden girl sits in her dirty diaper
she'll grow up a poet
loving suspension

You be the fat black crow

you be the driftwood

you be the poorest kid   dirty face

you be the crying one

you be the no name

strapped in
& spinning

At Carluccio's, County Dublin, Dawson Street

You know Beastie Boys?
the waiter says, in a thick Italian accent.
Yeah, I say, and he rolls
his bicep toward me:
Mike D, Adam Yauch (RIP), Adam Horovitz
in a boom box tattoo replete with
cross-hatched speakers.
I love them—you too? he says.
Yeah, I say,
my face close enough to kiss the Beasties in
full ink, 12 inches of American hip-hop
covering his arm on the corner of Dawson Street,
county Dublin, and I'm expecting him to
lean into "So What'cha Want":
"But like a dream I'm flowin
without no stoppin," but he says:
I want to go to America, but I can't,
his flashing eyes brown but
filled with light.
Maybe you will later,
I say—
Yes, yes, I will!
He takes the order, then all 5 ft. 8 inches
of muscle spring-steps to the kitchen,
his white shirt sleeve still half-
rolled to the speakers.
In those zones of the body
where lines are crossed—
he's crossing borders, but can't
leave his country.
So he needles his body black
with desire's music, and me sitting
in my leather jacket moving through space

with the ease of privilege, watching him.
In two days I'll fly
over the deep ocean.
He sets down the antipasta, leans in to me,
smiling: *You will do something big,*
I can smell it.
All his knives flashing, his arms tightening
with the lifting of the plates—
a good smell, he says—
the body's show, hard core,
lyrical.

Felon

Diamond Diner, 3 a.m.
He grabbed two pieces of white bread,
small in his thick hands, folded the bread
in two, scooping the eggs with one hand,
fried potatoes with the other. He worked both
hands like a machine, constant, like a generator.
His fleshy hands huge over the bread, forearms
and elbows on the counter. Head down,
bobbing a little when he scooped more food.
He didn't look up.
Whatsa matter, aren't you eatin? he said.
Were you ever in prison? I said.
He stopped, bread dripping egg in mid-air,
looked up at me with head still down.
Long black hair almost covering
his blue eyes metallic, beautiful.
Why you askin me that? he said.
I don't know, something about
the way you're eating.
Yeah, he said, *10–12, but I got out in 8.*
Eight years? I said, in this after-hours diner
with this guy I've been dancing with.
For what? I said.
Does it matter? he said, still scooping, still
bobbing, grabbing the napkin from the
table and wiping his mouth, crushing it
in a ball on the table.
He didn't give a fuck, and that's what
I wanted about him.
Yeah, it matters, I said.
We used to run drugs from Mexico,
fly em up here. We got caught.
You feel better now? he said.

Sure, I said, watching him scrape the plate
with his fork and knife at the same time,
two-handed, hard and noisy,
something more about light or wanting
to know what he knew—he was still
beautiful, watching him get everything he could
before shoving the plate away.
Ready to go? he said.

Armament

6 ft. 5 skinny guy on Castro Street,
leaping with arms thrashing a boom box
blasting "Crazy on You" by Heart and screaming:
Crazy   Crazy   Crazy
He slams the box over his head, then to his knees,
then kicking his legs up—*Crazy!*
His Einstein hair flying, then a spin,
twirling in a whacked-out dance.
A half block down, a young man
from the Southern Poverty Law Center
asks for $28, not sure why the exact amount—
while some guy in a raincoat's small chow-chow,
lion of the sidewalk with his blue-black tongue,
shits on the street in front of Café Mystique,
the guy running in circles yelling:
Get me a plastic bag!
Get me a plastic bag!
to no one.
A twelve year-old with white tee and round face,
about 50 lbs. overweight, holds a "Need Food" sign,
tilts his head back making mouth noises into the air:
Woooh! Woooh! Woooh!
Regular, every 5 seconds, like there's a timer
inside him.
I nod, he lets out a longer burst of air:
Woooooooooh!

Later, at the party on Market, a young guy says to me:
You can't wear body armor if you're a felon.
He says, *I like your rings. I used to wear steel-toed*
boots in high school. I look up at his half-Afro,
brown eyes. *You needed protection,* I say.

Yeah, yeah, I was bullied a lot, had to change schools.
I felt better with the boots.
Me, too, I say, holding my hands up: *These are good weapons.*
He and his boyfriend moved to a church basement
in the Mission after their racist landlord kicked them out:
We were getting beat up sleeping on the street,
so we crashed in the church for a while.
It's safe and there's no rent.
I'm thinking of safety and protection in 2020,
the big shield in the sky—
not god, but the Castro Theatre sign hanging down red
with huge white lettering:
"Raging Bull" is playing as the street
rages on every block:
in the air, between sidewalk cracks,
under the sewer grates,
and soon the streets will break in half,
the wildness taking its voice
to the storm lovers, the poor, the
dirtriders, into the deep heart of acquisition:
spilling into the high-end restaurants
and the stacked Victorians, just
a couple streets down where it's all cleaned up.
My friend says she doesn't even want
to hear about San Francisco since
the AIDS devastation—
the bathhouses just blocks away—
but the steam is everywhere.

The Pelicans

The pelicans are dive-bombing
off the coast of Sanibel in the Gulf of Mexico
& then gliding—
& I think of my sister's seamless attack,
then glide—
exactly like
the reincarnation of Timur
the Conqueror,
who built towers of his enemies' skulls.
Or Dylan's *ghost of Belle Starr*
(my sister's name at birth)
Star, what she always wanted
to be.
Sister, the ultimate slicer & dicer/
hero of her own mind—
I was the fly,
I was the fly
& like in "Tombstone Blues,"
everything unhinges:
"the sun's not yellow,
it's chicken."
With a blow torch she breathes through
me—
& I adore her,
I adore her.
I'm the willing, waiting one,
my body knowing no kin &
chained to her for dear life—
for a mere sense of what is dear.
The gulf is flat & serene now—
but underneath,
underneath.
Sister,

attack dog,
marking me
with the latest score,
my unlucky number.

The Fire Roads

We're sitting in a coffee shop
in Monroeville, PA—
site of Ed Ochester's amazing "asshole" poem,
when I say,
This is the place where I met my birthmother,
the third time.
In the wide dirt road of my heart,
only used in case of a bushfire,
now ride the deep mud, the roots sticking up:
I know the table—back, left.
She has on white capri pants, tan sandals, a blazing
orange top.
She's on fire
with what she knows and I don't—
the burning of my birth, and I push her:
You owe me this. I never
asked you for anything.
There's deadfall across the fire road,
washouts and runoff.
Nothing's marked.
She cries as my life opens
in this stupid, stupid coffee shop,
and Don says,
Oh my god—is she still alive?
I don't know, I say.
I'm trying to blast a singletrack,
and rockfall litters the path.
That's my family—I don't know
if my mother is alive or dead.
Don says,
I'm your family.
I know, I say, but feeling that pull
into the great cosmic sea and is

she still here?
And now the running kids
in the coffee shop—is it so hard
to know why I hate them?
In all this maze of backburning?
Their sharp, stabbing voices and
toy dinosaurs, but
worse, worse—
their fawning mothers and their
baby talk: *C'mon sweetie, pick up*
your toys so we can meet Daddy,
and my body flames up, fully involved,
and I want to scream at this vacant mother:
Put the goddamn dinosaur down,
this isn't your living room—
there is no living room.
I look at Don, his eyes blue, blue,
and blazing.
Is she dead? he says.
I'll look her up on the internet later, I say,
who the fuck knows—
the fire road burning inside us,
destroying our small heads and smaller dreams—
this burning we're all walking,
deadfall across a single track.

3

*Ride into the sunrise; the future
roars from the passing lane.*

Susan Stewart, "Inscriptions for Gas Pump TVs"

Coastal Starlite

I like the side life, what's happening out the window,
but I can feel it like it's in my body

We carry the bodies of all our failures inside us,
need to bury them, burn them

Surfers lined up in the water like little animal heads,
waiting for a wave   so beautiful

their vulnerability so painful
Go to Oceanside!   Right on the 101, a blink-

and-gone town   Pamela Anderson and her red
bathing suit could run out   to greet you

maybe just the suit
If you stay on the Coastal Starlite   you'll see

palm trees with crewcuts   a shiny black gate and
a guy will get on with a surfboard in a split pea green

soft case   the color of the sea on his planet
incredible light on the mountains and

burnt-out yurts on the beach   it's inevitable
that Neil Young sings in your headphones:

there was a fanfare blowing   to the sun
there was floating   on the breeze

Then you see the long piers   white wooden railings
and The Humming House Café

I don't want your redemption story—
I want some air

In resurrection, the men disappear into the smallness
of their ideas   and I was wrong so many times

but I keep being   with glimpses
of my former beautiful   incantations, incandescence

The Taos energy worker said:
you have an imprisoned heart

It's true that I always hated
the oblique nature of what some call   sophistication,

and I came to hate   what kept itself
from me   I wanted sovereignty

But now it's hot   in the underground canals, hot
in the body's river   in my mouth

in this traincar   Radiant field
light and dirt   all this burning

How I Became a Gunslinger

My mother was a horror movie.
I was afraid to meet her eyes because
they said, *disgust, send her back.*
I wanted too much, she said—this dress,
do it this way, those shoes, so I made myself dead
to be around her.
That was the only way:
I had to leave my body to stay.
My mother wasn't Frankenstein,
but the psych thriller where the betrayal
was organic, complete:
more like twisted doll heads,
stares from the dark corner of the room.
Even as a child I knew the words:
malice & intent.
She had them—this was no accident,
so I began making distinctions early:
was this the look of *Hush . . . Hush, Sweet Charlotte*
or the guise of *What Ever Happened to Baby Jane?*
My skills of dissolution served
me well: she birthed the gunslinger
in me, & *survive* became my battle cry.
So when I shot my first gun, a double-pump
Winchester, I found my true home.
It was just skeet, but I loved the feel
of the kickback, the bruise. The smell
of gunpowder in the western summer air;
the headache blazing for days;
I couldn't wait to feel the metal pump action
again, to point the barrel to the sky to
hit, to miss, but to shoot.
A feel like money in my hands—
like solid heart, complete—

the smell of dirt & leather,
& I didn't even know
what I was killing—
I just wanted it dead.

Speedballing

I woke bloody
    from snorting heroin,
        rocking myself skinless, the veins in my neck
        and my pink eyes speedballing blood

Shooting up words like all addicts do:
I never did heroin/I only snorted it
I never did crack/
I just free-based the coke I had

Getting clean a bigger mindfuck:
    Pray
    /they said
    /good/ they said
    let go/

They wanted blood for their spiritual path
and I wanted to please, but inside I was granular,
    weepy,

    I woke wanting frenzy—
    having never been trained in the sweet goodnight

When you ask yourself who's the animal,
who's the killer—
just know they taught us to drink the blood
of a man nailed to a cross. when we were children—

and so fuck it.
fuck sweetness, just fuck it
and every other misguided bedtime story,
    I skinned myself down/
    to my own idea of bone/

until the song and the gearshift became
my only true loves—
shooting up words to stay alive,

because
    everybody wants blood—it's just where and how
    you want to give it

Something Real and Free

for Don

I was reading a book about guitar players,
mostly Texas guys who loved Lightnin' Hopkins
and set themselves on the road to glory.
They talked poetry and jumping freighters,
bad gigs and bad years, and like Townes said,
We don't care about material stuff.
We want to hear the guitar ring one note correctly
and your voice ring the same note correctly
with the proper meaning correctly
for that instant.
I was running the streets too close to the sun,
I heard how good you were—that you played
slow blues, Chicago style, and burned the room up.
So I went to hear you in the concrete bunker bar
and through the beer and smoke and
the jesusdevil half-gone voices of the dive
it was a dog whistle from the underground, those
first notes you played. Clear and piercing,
like someone said later, a silver braid from
my heart to yours, and I don't
want to get soft, but the notes rang sweet and
true-hearted rough, and my head turned to face you, a man
inside that ringing, sending all that beauty
out into the night, and I recognized you—
felt your crushing hunger, your string-bending-
lowdown-full-body-badass love—
hitting that one note real and free—
doesn't matter who's watching
doesn't matter who's not
you and the Strat—
changing me
forever after, schooling me
in the ways of love.

Trumpcare

Hurt my leg in a fall,
think I need a wrap or x-ray,
but the white coat wants to prescribe Paxil.
He's writing a script, looking at his white pad,
I'm looking at his clean cut dark hair, his
boxy glasses moving and changing,
blurring him into an anteater head
or a politician.
I think this will help, he says,
his anteater tongue out and sliding.
What's my diagnosis? I say.
I didn't ask for medication, just told him about
my leg, my 79 cents-on-the-dollar body,
my woman-making-fuck-what-a-man-makes body—
65 cents for Black women/59 cents for Hispanic women,
he never looks up, says:
Take one of these at night.
Should I get an x-ray for my leg? I say,
his head now a big white box stuffed
with his high-end med school education.
He says: *Your diagnosis is unclear.*
I'm prescribing Paxil because
I can't really see you—
his foreclaws scratching and twitching,
his tongue covered in hooks.

Chocolate Mescaline

The woman in Detroit waits in line
to talk after the reading, her hair
in ringlets to her shoulders and hanging
bronze icons of women's bodies on her
firebrand dress. Maybe in her fifties,
she says: *I did chocolate mescaline last week—*
it was wonderful.
Oh, I say.
I directed it with my mind, she says,
I asked my therapist if I could start taking it.
He said no.
What do you think?
Can you see my crown chakra opening?
Can you tell me—
would acid be better for me?
What do you think?

Not Homeless, Just Moving

I wasn't homeless, just had my mattress
in my '69 Chevy, clothes underneath boxes

in the trunk. Everyday stuff in the front-seat
backpack. I moved 14 times that year,

drinking and drugs but still working
my waitress job. I was *in motion.*

Driving, working, hoping
to stay with a friend for a night,

I was pregnant but kept moving, and then
days later, fired from my downtown job

for trying to start a union—I wasn't—
just arguing a waitress policy.

So, the night before my abortion staying
with a bartender (not the father) on his couch,

his girlfriend came home late and rightly
kicked me out. I wasn't homeless,

just moving, 14 times that year,
and I was alone with it.

Borderlands, for Bobby

> . . . *there's no trace*
> *of the sky in the sky. I'll have to*
> *collapse the air to find you.*
>
> Sarah Messer

In this flat brown land, I can't find you—
it's so hot here, the Guadalupe Mountains flame up
with red dust and a town called Valentine
a half hour up the road—drive to Marfa Burritos,
Planet Marfa, and Marfa Pizza with brown workers
in 97 degree heat by the ovens, no air.

I'm up the road at the new hotel, comfortable while
riots in Memphis, Baton Rouge, St. Paul after
police shootings last week. Where am I in this?
One year before the El Paso massacre and
the world ring of turquoise you gave me,
on my finger for years, the silver loosening.

I'm going to Moonstone, the Marfa rockshop today
to see if I can find you, because the sun
isn't giving you up. The sprawling clouds almost
blue with the sky, I
think you are flying between worlds,
am I making all of this up?

Sunday in El Paso, so much Spanish and
almost everyone is brown-skinned.
I'm one of the only people with blonde hair (dyed)
but feel at home, no one staring at me
like they do in small town airports
like Sheridan or Laramie.

You can see hanging laundry from
the airport runway, patches of color strung
house-to-house, but harder now to cross
the border from Juárez. Drought-brown
Franklin Mountains fix the sightline:
housing   freeway   trains   border

On Rt. 90, I think I see a white whale in the distance.
Traveling 12 hours, I know something is tethered to
the brown ground—what is it?
Closer, it looks like a rounded, cartoony airplane,
am I hallucinating? In the high desert, they say if you
don't hydrate, your mind spins out.

I keep driving, find out next day
it's a surveillance blimp for drug trafficking—
and later we see a drug bust on Highland Avenue,
2 Texas State Troopers corral a pickup, slashing
side panels, lights flashing. 2 brown boys in cuffs
on the curb. They say a major drug run from the border.

Dirt, dust cattle ranches—
it's unforgiving here but so
beautiful in its straightforward lines—
dirt,
house,
sky.

You can get anything you want here:
skull teeshirts, vintage GTOs clean as old money.
Donald Judd everywhere. Meet Ray the Aries guitar player
in his orange plaid cowboy shirt, maybe the most
real of all. Add some flames and you've got
a goddamn scenario.

Used-to-be ranches, old-style windmills.
You can live in a yurt or a tipi,
get tea with marijuana tincture, Marfalafel,
Early Grey chocolate chip cookies, and
everything that tastes like something else.
What you can't find is a sandwich.

Bobby, if I could find you,
I'd say, *hello*, and *how is your new life?*
Are you resting or flying?
Maybe both at once.
The guy at the rock shop doesn't love rocks.
I ask him: *Is Marfa agate for grounding?*

He says, *That's what they say.*
Do you believe in this stuff? I ask.
No, he says.
I didn't think so, I say.
5 years since you died,
and we're all still missing you:

your head down, holding a rock like it's the first time,
always your brown eyes alive, happy
as you lift your head.
I'm still here, asking the same questions.
There are flames.
Change, you would say, a lot of change coming.

Yellow Sky

The summer that I had nowhere to live:

the sky was yellow everywhere.
The cars of other people had their own private shine.

I walked slowly.
Several birds re-visited the backyards of strangers,

I was free
singing the song of the last thing I didn't say to you.

For the Man Who Died on the Tracks

Edmonton, British Columbia
June 30, 1987

For the man who died at 10 p.m.,
walking the train tracks in the late June dark,
to you:

Can I tell you that we mourned?
The stewards cried, the conductors joked
to hide their fright, the children in coach saw
your body fly by at dusk in the Canadian night.

We stared. I prayed. I read a poem
by Gary Snyder to Alan Watts in memory
of his death, for I didn't know your name,
though someone said you were a man
of forty-five.

And I don't know if you walked along
the tracks to die and why
you didn't jump at the whistle?
But I want to tell you that a baby cries

right now, 45 minutes later and the whistle
is blowing longer now
and more often.
It sounds like a cry, a wall

of death and people sit in their rooms,
doors open, and stare, and say
how sad it is.

I think of my dead father and ask him
to help you. I want you to know
that you are mourned.
I sit in a cabin and talk of my dad

and listen to the steward speak of
the death of his grandparents and his
love for them.

I want you to know
that we stopped and prayed and we
cried for you, you the forty-five-
year-old man on the tracks on

June 30, 1987 in the Canadian night.
Gerrie, the train steward, said,
"I don't know how to feel."
We looked for your body.

The sirens came.
We stood on the back of the train
with the steam rising and hoped
for your life.

We looked through binoculars, we
looked at each other,
we stopped and mourned.

4

*Fog. Railroad
crossing at the
end of the world.*

Earl Keener

Containment

Containment. In this train compartment, the stainless steel breaks at an angle, hangs sharp. With the bunk down, there's enough room to turn around if you lift your leg strategically. Yet, I love this containment. Being *inside* of something. A pod. Not wide enough to stretch both arms out—10 ft. long. 2 x 4 mirror, 3 x 4 window, narrow storage shelf near the ceiling. Packed in like a dog, a fish—safe. I'm back in some womb? Back in the attic with the hatch closed after me. Containment as escape?

Bolt on the door—no way on or off the train all day as we wind through Canada. Why does this imprisonment feel like freedom and vice versa? I take pictures of the light switch, a silver toggle; slide the weight-bearing lever to lower the bunk/repeat: the scraping metal, the clamp and safety latch at the foot. The design flawless and comforting.

Freedom. The train runs 10 hours late, nothing works. Knowing no one. Give me this room, a place—some books and my lover. I'm tired of arranging, talking—all the useless choices. I'll see you next lifetime.

The train stopped for the last 20 minutes/we are here. More here than usual. I love to be stopped, to be in that moment of nowhere/on the way to/but not going now/—what is that?

Waiting in the midst of motion, the million small minutes of it that will never be remembered—but experienced fully. Stored, where? Wifi not working. Phone not working—we are actually full-body. Breathing, feeling *here*.

Landing Strip—Sierra Nevada

6:35 p.m. 4/14/17

Where the Sierra Nevada run into crop circles,
landing strip with cloud cover & then
the moon water. The mountain folds
look like a brown blanket bunched,
then the edge & a massive valley.

6 circles & dust/then 6 more.
Looks like a lake bed from before
the dinosaurs. Spiny white-topped ridges
in the distance. Low ranges rising
up again, that Western dirt-brown you

can't see or feel anywhere else—home.
Small glacial lakes in distance.
So many shapes, uprising, mounds.
Roads crossing like chalklines
through the mountains.

Every now & then,
a white moving thing—
probably a semi, but looks like
a crawling bug from the high-up plane.
Scale is gone.

Mountain shadows form a double
mountain/the backs of bison,
prehistoric & sleeping. Mounds
of sandstone, sediment, alive &
splitting into fissures & now

so much snow. Soft-looking white
next to the jagged peaks.

There is magic everywhere.
Now another valley, sea
of brown—massive body.

Who built these roads threading through?
What first bodies, what brave hearts,
slave labor doing the impossible?
I am smaller now.
Big holes like rocketships landed.

A huge circle of silver & panels &
blue pools on the side.
What is it?
Looks like a solar project or spaceship
docking station.

In the middle of desert.
Every shape looks like a glacier path—
dry now. See the force & direction
of what once was—in the valley
and rock remains.

Now looks like something that used to be
waterfall, or maybe is in winter with
snowmelt. Striations, sensual folds of brown rock.
Now water   green   glacial   lake   huge
exhilaration of mountains

landing strip

Train-Jumper

Interview, Moundsville Penitentiary, 1975

I used to love jumpin trains, he said.
That's how I got this, he knocked on
his wooden stick leg, old school like
Captain Ahab he said, with a broom handle-
like extension that rose from knee to waist.

The stilt sticking out of his pant leg
below the knee, and gathered up and above it,
like it was stuffed with sheets or cotton or
something soft, and when he walked,
his whole body shook as he swung

his right peg leg around in a half-
circle, enough to power a generator.
About 5 ft. 6 and skinny, with years
on his face in deep cuts of wrinkles
and dark circles of eyes. Sitting in

the visitor room of Moundsville
Penitentiary, he said: *I threw a rock*
through the window of the pawn shop
to get a gun, robbed the 7-11 next door.
All I took was an Orange Crush

and a beef jerky. Didn't take long.
I sat on the curb until the cops came—
was the best beef jerky cause I knew
I was comin back. This is home now.
I'm too old for the trains.

Here's good.

Field

The graffitied walls north of Anaheim,
then a stop, army-barrack-looking houses,
huge compost piles,
Fullerton.
Amtrak 763 Northbound,
trucks, trucks, plugged into walls to unload,
and old friends are changing shape.
I'm making models of people I used to know—
out of coffee and cayenne.
What is the opposite of open arms?
Earthmovers are fenced in at the trainyard,
with trees along the perimeter.
Chainlink chainlink, and we're slowing
to San Pedro Junction, where compacted trash
is truck-size and seagulls sweep the rails.
That process of interchange with new people
is exhilarating, shocking the body awake
into why am I here now?
And old friends are like train graveyards,
stopped for washing and repair under
huge coverings, in open hangars.
The cold storage of so many sins?
Too many days from the old city?
Still, and always, the foothills are magnificent.
Send out the sad songs:
Field, where is your new heart?
Are you building the house inside the body now?
Or are there too many drowned trees?

At Moe's

I was reading at Moe's on Telegraph,
legendary Berkeley bookstore praised
by the *San Francisco Chronicle*:
"India has the Taj Mahal, Berkeley has Moe's Books."
There was a Beyoncé concert in San Francisco
that night, so the crowd was thin but rabid
with book buying, and Joyce Jenkins of *Poetry Flash*
beamed her spirit light everywhere.
Richard Silberg said,
I saw your flame self rise up when you read. It was
large and beautiful.
Wow. Thanks, I said, and thought of
the cool history of the place, founded by
anarchist Moe Moskowitz, home to People's Park
and the Free Speech Movement,
happy to read my dirty poems there.
I thought of my "real" name
with the initials P.S.:
not a post script,
but more a year in the asylum,
a handoff—
the body's cave, the more
that's coming.

Outpost on Wicklow Street

for Sean O'Reilly

In this outpost of empire,
I celebrate my own bronze age,
preparing my tools:

organic verse my choice
for how the dream world comes
into the daily air.

There are voices on my arms
and legs, there are voices coming
out of me that are not mine—

when I talk, the deep hole
of the seven nights *cracks*
and there is the rocky path

to the first lightpost.
Take it.
Take it to the first words I ever heard:

(orphanage voices: strangers   nuns   killers
missionaries   prison guards   pedophiles)
all living inside me

Now the night air my curious director,
now this new continent of sound:
making me look up to the black ink

of sky/
look down at the dirt, endless
dirt between cobblestones on Wicklow in

County Dublin—
and know/
but don't know how, who

spoke me here,
the voices that spiked me
alive.

Driver: Fulton Street to North Beach

10 p.m. on a Friday, I jump in.
The cab driver looks straight ahead:

I've been looking up houses
we used to live in when I was small—
I found them on Google Earth—
not sure why—just wanted to look at them.

Maybe you need to go back and get something? I say.

We were dirt poor, he says.
Never had enough milk to last the week.
I don't know why I'm telling you this.

I've been dreaming, he says.

I used to wake up crying when I was a kid—
6 yrs old—and tell my mother I was sad that
she and my father were going to die.

You must have been worried, I say.

She always said:
that's not going to be for a long time,
now go to sleep.

He squints into the mirror, then turns
to look intently at me with oversized aviator glasses:

Do you think dreams are real? he says.
Do you think dreams make sense?

In the Castro

I met a friend of RuPaul's on Market & Noe—
he told me how much he loved Phyllis Hyman
and Primanti's—that's all he knew about Pittsburgh.

Phyllis was an amazon, he said,
graceful and sophisticated in her performance.
She killed herself years ago, I'm not sure what year.

He had gem-like blue eyes, a shaved head.
His muscled body about 5 ft. 6 in a tight
button-up light blue jersey shirt.

He said, *You know she suffered from manic depression.*
In person she swore like a trucker &
her grace disintegrated.

A friend of mine was waiting to see her in San Francisco
at the BRAVA! Theater with a stack of albums,
and he obviously was suffering from AIDS &

she wouldn't acknowledge him, kept talking
to her friends, until her friends said:
Phyllis, please.

And without skipping a beat, in one motion
she took each album & scrawled
her name without looking at him.

He said he wished he never met her—
her grace could've stayed intact.
She never even looked at him.

Kat Calls about Jesus

I was up all night last night and I can't decide, she says.
Her voice gravelly but spiking high.
I want to talk about whether Jesus
is the son of God, she says.
At the Oregon Coast, I'm trying
to get away—
there's nothing like the blue-grey of the ocean sky
just before dark.
You know I don't believe it, I say,
a bunch of stories written by men to control people.
Yeah, but do you think Jesus is the Son of God? she says.
I tell her: *Well, if you're talking about the structure of it,*
like who's in charge, like a family business—
sure, I guess so.
What do YOU think? I say.
I think Jesus Christ is the Son of God.
Great, I say, *it's settled.*
I hate the voices in her head and what they do
to her, hate myself for not wanting to listen.
There's nothing like the blue-grey of the ocean sky
just before dark.—and this dark,
this back and forth means nothing—
voices in her head/voices in mine.
I don't know anything—
not the reason Kat's mind takes her swimming
to Jesus,
not the reason I agree to talk about it—
Except I wish maybe *saying it*—
whatever it is—could shift the axis of the world right again.
But it never does, it never works and
the waves crash all night and
the next day I'm ridiculous,

calling out to the sea
and the swell of spirits—
looking out this window believing
in water.

She Was West

I hadn't yet met my flame self,
my life was a topographical dictionary,
bumps & rises, steep canyons.
I was looking for the spiking sun—
I could feel the formations, but not as mine.
The massive dictionary a foot thick
inside me with red leather cover & silver rivets
holding me together. Read it & keep it
in my clothes closet—pull it out at night
until the cover falls off, pages torn &
so thick I can never exhaust it & always
more room for me, a way to leave home—
the green encyclopedias I stored in
my body: Funk & Wagnall's & I
read them, hungry for knowing what was
out there: the countries, world, the
desert flowers, the miracle times
of the body & mind:
I met her in 1983,
Martha West.
I was sitting on the rounded curb,
side road in Tucson by the dirt garden.
Looking at the sky for answers, crying
at my life & she drove up
in a little red car:
Do you need help?
Yes, & I jumped in.
I'm on my way to an AA meeting—want to go?
Sure, I said, anywhere to not be with myself.
We went on like that for weeks,
her driving/me sitting.
She was a working *National Geographic* photographer,
& it was April. The desert was in bloom.

She took me to lunch
she showed me the flowers in the desert
& to her place, a small adobe with paned windows
& inside rooms sheeted off—with colorful scarves &
spreads, a table with a cloth draped over it,
everything attended to, adorned with color.
She fed me fruit & a sandwich, fresh juice,
carrot ginger, everything I had never had.
I was lost, I was opening to her.
She said, You can stay with me, you don't
have to go home.
Martha West said BE HERE NOW, said—
You are whole—
She was my new dictionary, with words
& flash canyons & infant streams.
She showed me how to fold my body up &
let it go—
to speak with words about pain—
always hidden.
She was sent to the world & I
walked with her for a while—
some people open the world for you
like a flash inevitable,
she was West.
She was ageless, sun in her face, 50s maybe,
alive with saying what was on her mind,
splitting the world open.
It was a time, an unfolding—
a flash field where dirt ruled &
the tracks through the desert became
my tracks through the body—
and transforming, wild running love.
Dirt, dirt, splitting open the body

where streams cut a path—
I don't know if it was gold poppies,
paperflowers, or Indian blanket—
flowering this hot April, & Martha, the sender—
said some once every 20 years & now,
alive.
Brought by a triggering rain,
these colors other than I've seen
everything other than I've seen.
Dirt, the tunneling in & down—
the lifting up—break through—
BE HERE NOW.
You are perfect & whole,
she said—
words never heard & another
language in this new encyclopedia:
I could never walk steady as myself.
& all my former dead selves walked
the dirt & felt it dust up on us
as Paradise.

5

The hills of glass, the fatal brilliant plain.

Muriel Rukeyser, *The Book of the Dead*

Beautiful, Overused in Muir Woods

Sitting in the cathedral trees, the air full
of water & more air—
almost liquid air—
sweet against the skin, the wide planks
of the great American platforms
for the people to walk & many benches,
Green! Green!
Water running west—with the massive
fallen tree parts crossing,
families of all languages:
Japanese, Arabic, German, picture taking,
the canopy of the tallest above us,
no better covering—
I want to weep for the comfort,
the peace of it
tree love everywhere
—moss, lichen—
hanging decomposing branches that
have become their new beauty:
thick spindles next to the giant thick
Redwoods,
cut the tree down, see
the years.
Don't cut the tree, feel
the years.
We are small, small, thank god for
the smallness
and love is big,
and I'm meeting Pierre, the taxi driver,
at 2—*Be there*
by the blocked entrance where those guys
are standing—be on time! he says,
Give me some money, he says.

He's listening to a broadcast on his phone
from Haiti, his home.
Go there, he says, *you will have something
to write—the water, the land,
is beautiful.*
All we hear is trouble, I say.
Trouble, no trouble, Pierre says, turns
his thin face toward me, missing
most of his front teeth.
The love pouring off of him like
tree air, like seedlings, running
streams—
You give me tip? he says,
Oh, yeah, I say.
Ok.
The tree hut holds millions of years,
demarcated.
Read the tree.
Read about the tree.
Go up close, feel
the fucking tree, my god,
I am lucky,
we are
this beautiful strangled world.
The Germans are laughing in their
grey sweaters, the Japanese argue
about the age of the tree, now
the German men pose
in grey sweater vests, just the men
against the tree, hurry—get the picture.
Pierre in leather jacket & jeans, black
hat that says: Brixton Supply, and dramatic
green hills, all trees, we're listening to

'90s pop, Abba—he says: *Look, Eucalyptus.*
I can't tell you how thrilling.
We are in this together, this *watching
inside of*, and a few modern houses perched
on these hillsides. *Who lives there?* I say.
Pierre says, *You could buy one, a bit
of money*, and I see his white goatee
for the first time as we pass Muir Meadows
and Christina Aguilera's singing, *I am beautiful/
No matter what they say/Words can't
bring me down*, and she's from Pittsburgh and
everyone nailed her for being trashy and
dirty and I say, *She's doing it her way*,
onto the S curves, the winding, Pierre needs
some oil, we stop at a Mill Valley station
and he says, *I have to make the money
to pay for the car. I need to make $100/day
for the car, and then some for me, when
Obama was in, it was better.
Sometimes I make it/sometimes I don't.*
And I think of the beautiful Doug Powell,
how the next day I tell him about Pierre
and the trees, and Doug says, *The blue gum
eucalyptus have these beautiful oval shapes
and then they become falciform,*
and if you know Doug, you know his
brilliant, esoteric love of everything,
and he tells me the leaves become hard and
sickle-shaped, and I think of Pierre,
and Doug, and me,
of us all meeting over trees,
our spirits spinning around the magic West.

It's Raining in Paterson

Poetry reading at my father's grave,
Queen of Heaven cemetery, and I'm kneeling
on garbage bags on the rain-soaked ground.
He never heard me read, but would the poems
slide through?
To that other world—is it there?

He would laugh, say,
I shoulda never sent you to college.
Which, in his working-class language, meant:
I'm proud of you.
And I'm reading out loud, my gardenia poem,
    the lines that make no sense/the beautiful abandonment

Crying and everything wet—
and now it's thirty years gone,
raining in Paterson, New Jersey, flooding
in Hoboken, and I'm thinking of my husband
at home, how I'll hold him at night and
talk to the slide-through world—

not in poems, but in rains of supplication—
Keep him safe, and *Thank you*
to my father, now spirit guide, yes.
Saying yes to this beautiful life
of gardenias, their wide open vowels
and goodnight.

She only tried a little, unwound the coat hanger and put it inside her

She only tried a little, unwound the coat hanger and put it inside her. There was a lot of blood, he said. When my birthmother tried to give herself an abortion, he said she used a coat hanger to try to cause a "miscarriage." She was desperate, he said, and panicking about being pregnant and what would she do, she had no money, couldn't raise a baby.

But, who was he? I didn't trust him, his name was on my birth certificate, but who was he, really? He said: *She only tried a little, unwound the coat hanger and put it inside her.* Was he there? He said she pushed inside with it a few times, and the bleeding started, and then she stopped. There was a lot of blood, he said, and she thought that she would "miscarry," but it never happened. After that, she hid herself in the upstairs bedroom and waited.

I never asked her about that story. But I wondered if it was true. I believe it is, and in thinking about it, I struggled to imagine what it might have felt like from the inside of her body.

My Father Disappears into Flowers

The apple tree in the backyard with white waterfall blossoms:

my father's body disappearing in his sickness down to 90 lbs,
his hat floating on his head:

my father falling into the clothes rack trying to buy
smaller pants to fit—

he's not gone

The air heavy with waterfall, and him—
vaulting down the front steps in spring:

Hot in the Striped Boy's Heart

It's hot in the loading bridge,
hot in the birth canal,
it's hot in the striped boy's heart—
we're two women driving to D.C. for an abortion
in my beater sea-green LeMans with the SEX,
DRUGS, AND ROCK 'N' ROLL sticker on the bumper.
It's hot living in my car with the mattress
in the back, the windshield wipers disintegrating
and so it's raining all the way to D.C. and
my friend is terrified, let it go too long
with a guy she loves but he could care and
she can't face her parents. Borrowed money
from the waitresses we worked with,
saline solution for a second trimester abortion,
it's hot in the Silverman's teeshirt I'm still
wearing from sixth grade with gold and blue stripes,
hot in the men's store buying my first real shirt
with my girlfriend Patty. I was a boy then, not
yet a woman following the sightlines
from the silver hood ornament to the double yellow.
Hot in the Pontiac trunk of clothes and boxes and
the cheap hotel in Silver Springs for the early
morning procedure, two women in their twenties
out of state for treatment, hot in this traveling altar,
these bodies run amok. Body of light, body
of doubles. Body of never telling anyone, never
seeing her again. Hot in my striped boy's heart
in this car dragging home with no talk,
still bleeding.

On the 101

An atlas on the underside of my dream
Jennifer Elise Foerster

On the cab ride from the San Francisco airport,
the driver a guy named Thom from Southeast Asia.
Are you in town for convention? he says,
No, I say, *I'm a poet, I'm here to write.*
His face changes in the rearview,
he gets that look in his eye,
that flash/then retreat I've seen so often.
Are you a writer? I say.
Oh, no, no, he says, *I work on English.*
You seem like a writer to me, I say.
He smiles, *I study. In my country, is hard to get education.*
I have done middle school.
He grabs 3 books from the passenger seat, lifts them up:
This is what I do. I read these books.
I talk to people, way to learn.

The cab fills with moving air, my face waking cool
to the cirrus sky.
Wow, I say, *That's great,*
it seems like a really good way to do it—
can I see those books?
His face opens, his brown eyes alive, and he
passes them back to me.
They're written in a language I've never seen.
This Burmese, he says, *my language.*
These books I read to learn.
I've never seen books like these, I say.
Yes, he says,
these are my books.
Great, I say,
as I hand them back to him.

We're driving by the San Francisco Bay,
I feel opened to the air and the great expanse.
Can I find my way to my birthfather,
poems of where I came from?
Thom hands me one of the books and says,
Gift for you.
Surprised, I say,
Oh, my—
and look at the slim green book:
the cover a waterfall with rose-colored flowers.
The cover and inside written in Burmese.
It is Buddhist book.
I am Buddhist, he says.
This is very kind of you, I say,
and Thom nods.

I don't think I should keep this, I say,
I don't know how to read it,
and this is one of your books.
Maybe one day you learn, he says, smiling.
I'm nodding,
yes, he's right,
Yes, you're right, I say,
I can learn like you're learning.
Thank you, thanks so much.
I knew I wouldn't learn the language, but
I'd read it, I'd feel the voices moving through me
as I held the book.
Thom is very happy and saying,
My gift to you,
and I thank him again.

The bay still there, blue with its endless stories and upheavals.

I say, *When we get there, I want to give you one of my books.*

Thom's face tightens,

No, no, not that. I give you MY book. My gift.

I see I've upset him and say,

I know, I appreciate your gift.

But I want to give you one of my books too as a gift.

He looks at me in the rearview, his eyes serious,

as if he's checking me for truth.

Okay. Okay, he says.

Thank you, I say.

I open the green book.

It's all written in Burmese, with the exception

of about 10 numbered sentences in English.

I open to the first English sentence:

    1. You will be given a body.

Leaving Sioux City

for Marcella Redmund

I don't know what I'd do if I couldn't go outside
in my pajamas and look at the sky, Marcella says.
3 a.m. wake-up call & a 4:15 pickup
to head to the airport. I'm drugged up
with codeine for influenza B, amazed that
she can both talk & drive. Headed from Vermillion
to Sioux City, & what light from Marcella's
heart? It outshone her headlights.
5:30 a.m. at the airport, a large woman in sweatpants
& furry clogs checks her little cat, Peanut, onto
the flight. It takes 15 minutes while a string
of 12 people wait in line behind her.
Goodbye, Peanut! she cries, blows a kiss &
shuffles away. The attendant at American Airlines
says to her: *I'm sorry this took so long.*
That's okay, she says, *more time with my Peanut,*
oblivious to the line behind her.
At the Blue Sky Café, open at 4, a woman with
bushy grey hair & sweatshirt says,
Can I help you?
Can I have one of those teeshirts that say SUX? I say.
Sure, you know that's for Sioux City? she says,
but I was thinking it was short for "sucks."
Full of codeine from the polite South Dakota doctor,
I'm staring.
Where you from? she says.
Before I can answer, she explains:
About a mile from here, you can stand on a hill
& see three states.
I stare at her quizzically.
Nebraska, Iowa, South Dakota, she says.
Oh, Nebraska, I say, not knowing it was next door.

Yep, she says, *just turn around in a circle &*
see all three. Too bad you're leaving, she says,
carefully folding & smoothing my SUX teeshirt.
I guess I'll have to come back, I say.
She smiles, *It's something to see. Have a*
great prairie weekend, she says, miraculously
at 5:45 a.m., & after Peanut, after influenza B,
I am in love again—spinning.

Kat Talks the War Inside Her

    She says:
I found the connection—River
was shooting heroin, which, if you think
about it, is a river of chocolate or maybe
it's one of the golden tickets to the factory,
and Johnny was really Charlie, not
the original Willy.

Kat not taking her pills again, she wants
to know who the real Johnny Depp is—
the one who owned the Viper Room,
whose band played the night River Phoenix
died outside
                or is he really
Willy Wonka? But then, Kat says,
I thought Gene Wilder was the real Willy,
because Johnny left town after the
Halloween overdose, and Willy,
he would never, ever
leave a friend, even after
they're dead.

    I say:
Why don't you start your meds again,
they might help you with this.

    No, she says,
I got it figured out.
It's the trees.
The gumdrop trees, the candy mountains
and the glass elevator.

The Saddest Song

after Townes Van Zandt

If "Tecumseh Valley" is the saddest song ever written,
and if I'm writing out of my heart, and if

Townes really meant that . . . *sunshine walked beside her*,
then we're all fucked, and we are—

and if

her dreams were denied / Her pa had died,
then I'm saying there's no season that's right

for dying, there's no weight that the heart
can make light, and I'll never see you again.

In the Lowfields

1.

We are not in the world now—
only riding through it
with the bending trees
on their way out.
We're on our way too.

The discarded have so much
to say to us, yes.
Yes, the blue shirt on the grass—
but I'm sick of visiting the reflecting pool.

This bending:
Look. We're between you
and nothingness.
We used to blanket you with borders.
Now we're on our way to make
a carpet for your feet
as you walk away.

Check: snowy egret
          in the mud banks—
          the drainage ditch—
          luminous

Blue grey sky   air currents
    turbulent   shifting

Still more light extending,
half-built sheds with blue tarp.
Time opens into the present.

Let the world in
Let the world in

2.

The blinding beauty of the student
who wants to write her life.
She said, *In the dream, the cherubs
surrounded me. They said I was fading away,
that it would never be like it was.*

Currents in the room, and she
looked at me with deep brown eyes.

Dream it again, I said.
*The angels are coming, they're around you
right now.*

And they were.
She let me hold them for a minute.

3.

In the lowfields.
In the rolling green fields of your arms,
I live.

There needs to be an accounting.
For the way the trees bend and slump.
And me—bandit of my own life—
I'm wishing for a new manifold of sky and
knowing I'm lacking.

My dreams tell me everything we knew before
was broken.
My dreams tell me dream it again.

West Texas Love Poem

Spread a map on the hood of your car
and try to remember what you wanted.
If you want to be seen as yourself, that
might not happen.
If you wanted the prize, the explosion,
the magnificence—
Run your hands over the map, feel
the softness of the paper, the engine heat
through the Guadalupe Mountains.
Nobody promised you anything,
and they shouldn't have.
The mint green of the old map
catapults you home, home
meaning wherever your hand is.
The topographical blue lines make you
long for old highs and lows,
like they were something,
well—they got you here,
to this car, this life.
Straighten the corners near West Texas,
remember how goddamn lucky you are
to be loved,
now get in the car
and drive.

NOTES

"Stormday" makes use of lines from John Muir's book *A Wind-Storm in the Forests*, American Roots Series, 2014.

"Gunlover" includes lines after the work of Bruce Weigl, and with thanks.

"Drunken Trees" refers to the tilting of trees in subarctic environments such as Alaska and parts of Canada. This occurs due to the melting of the permafrost due to climate change. The poem's epigraph is a quote from Sarah James, a Native American Elder who lives in Arctic Village in northeastern Alaska. "Drunken Trees: Dramatic Signs of Climate Change," Brian Clark Howard, *National Geographic*.

"The Pelicans" refers to some lines in Bob Dylan's song "Tombstone Blues" from *Highway 61 Revisited*.

"The Fire Roads" refers to Ed Ochester's widely anthologized poem, "Monroeville, PA," from his book *Miracle Mile*, Carnegie Mellon University Press, 1984.

"Coastal Starlite" was written while riding the Coastal Starlight from San Diego to San Francisco. It makes use of some lines from Edward Abbey.

"Something Real and Free" makes use of a quote from Townes Van Zandt from *I'll Be Here in the Morning: The Songwriting Legacy of Townes Van Zandt*, (John and Robin Dickson Series in Texas Music, sponsored by the Center for Texas Music History, Texas State University) Brian T. Atkinson, 2011.

"Borderlands, for Bobby" is for Bobby Patak, beloved friend and rock lover who dug rocks all over the world before his death in 2010.

"Containment" was written on the VIA Rail Canadian from Toronto to Jasper.

"Train-Jumper" references my brief work as a social worker in Mounds-ville Penitentiary for Project 60, a program designed to help long-term inmates design a "life plan" for themselves upon release.

"Field" was written while riding the Coastal Starlight from San Diego to San Francisco. It includes a variation on lines from "Lazaretto" by Jack White.

"She Was West" makes reference to the iconic book BE HERE NOW, by Ram Dass, the self-proclaimed American yogi and spiritual leader of the seventies. Born as Richard Alpert, he was known for his association with Timothy Leary and their drug experimentation at Harvard.

"West Texas Love Poem" makes use of a variation of lines from Terry Tempest Williams, with thanks.

ACKNOWLEDGMENTS

The author wishes to acknowledge the following journals in which some of these poems first appeared, sometimes in earlier versions:

Cherry Tree ("At Carluccio's," "Stormday"); *Cold Mountain Review* ("For the Man Who Died on the Tracks," "Kat Calls About Jesus," "Yellow Sun"); *Copper Nickel* ("Crushing It"); *Florida Review* ("She Was West"); *Gulf Stream* ("Double-Cut," "Not Homeless, Just Moving"); *HeArt* ("Speedballing"); *New England Review* ("Field," "The Body Wars"); *Nomadic Ground* ("Fulton St. to North Beach"); *Paterson Literary Review* ("In the Castro" "Leaving Sioux City," "Outpost on Wicklow Street," "Sierra Nevada—Landing Strip," "West Texas Love Poem"); *Pedestal Magazine* ("At Moe's," "Kat Talks the War Inside Her"); *Pleiades* ("My Father Disappears into Flowers"); *San Diego Poetry Annual* ("Borderlands, for Bobby," "Coastal Starlite," "Containment," "Driver: Fulton St.," "Felon," "How I Became a Gunslinger," "The Fire Roads"); *Shrew* ("Something Real and Free"); *2 Bridges* ("The Saddest Song"); *World Literature Today* ("Hot in the Striped Boy's Heart")

The author also wishes to acknowledge the following anthologies where poems have appeared:

Across the Waves: New Poems from Ireland and the U.S., edited by Jean O'Brien and Gerry LaFemina. County Clare, Ireland: Salmon Poetry, 2020 ("Stormday," "At Carluccios").

What Saves Us: Poems of Outrage and Empathy in the Age of Trump, edited by Martín Espada. Evanston, IL: Northwestern University Press, 2019 ("Trumpcare").

I would like to express my appreciation to the Pennsylvania Council on the Arts; the Pittsburgh Cultural Trust and the Howard Heinz Endowment and Laurel Foundation; the Pittsburgh Foundation; the Creative Capital Foundation; the Brush Creek Ranch Residency; the MacDowell Colony; Allison Adelle Hedge Coke and the Platte River Whooping Crane Trust; The Poetry Center, Passaic County Community College; Santa Fe Arts Institute; Ucross; and Leighton Studios, Banff, Alberta,

Canada for fellowship and support that helped me to write these poems. Special thanks to the wonderful staff at the University of Pittsburgh Press, especially David Baumann for continued commitment, expertise, and good humor; Alex Wolfe for great editing; Joel W. Coggins for killer cover design; Chloe Wertz for good-hearted publicity; John Fagan and Kelly Thomas for enthusiastic marketing. Big thanks to Michael Lotenero for his brilliant painting, *insidemymind*; with gratitude to Beth Kukucka for inventive photography over the years.

Whole-hearted thanks to the following people who have helped me with these poems: Ed Ochester for seeing into poems and his brilliant, one-of-a-kind advice; Judith Vollmer, treasured companion on this wild road, for wolf vision that helped to imagine this book; D. A. Powell for great humanity and giving me poems when he talks; Tracy K. Smith for exceptional kindness and going deep; Sandra Cisneros for singular courage and candles and the chocolate; Sapphire for going beyond brave; Diane Glancy, seer, for showing the way; Sharon Hawkins at Brush Creek for saving me, for the ride, the cooler, over-the-top kindness; Dr. Ruby Lee for the drugs and good talk; Martin Farawell for his heart-felt poems that will tear you up; Denise Duhamel, kick-ass poet and feminist; Julie Marie Wade for saying it true; Lee Ann Roripaugh for lunch in Laramie and scary poems; Richard Blanco, inaugural human for his generous spirit(and biceps); Allison Adelle Hedge Coke, sister, for her revolutionary ways; Kayla Sargeson for freaky poems and giving life to Deanie; Tess Barry, relentless Sagittarian, for facials and her beautiful work and Thom for their immeasurable kindness; my hair-dresser, Erika, for the Yellow; Zoe at the Santa Fe rock shop, for cosmic encounters; Maria Mazziotti Gillan, poet of poets, for the best swearing and paintings; Nancy Kirkwood, bloodsister, actually forthcoming; David Groff for tough poems and New York talks; Anne Rashid for *The Country in You;* Tony Trigilio, for the shadows and love of all things eerie; William Harry Harding for San Diego dinner and bringing life to poems;

Heather Donohue for cosmic stories; 8th Street Rox for poem vibes; Patty McCollum, kindest of all, for the heart music; Joan Bauer, connector, world poet; George Guida for big-hearted poems and galactic Danville; Tim Green for the almost *Rattle* reading in Wrightwood; Wendy Scott Paff for her unrelenting poems; John Amen for carrying on; Lori Wilson for *The Dream Women Called*; Beatrice Vasser for saying the hard truth; Nancy Koerbel for original wildness; Rigoberto Gonzalez for brave memoir and killer shoes; Peg Alford Pursell for *Why There Are Words*; Nicole Santalucia for boob art and poems-on-fire; Suzanne Roberts for loving the road; Lynn Emanuel, slasher and poet of edge and grace; James Allen Hall for fearless writing and Casbah talk; David Trinidad for his generous answer; Afaa Michael Weaver for good jokes and keeping it real; Gerry LaFemina for years of friendship and the Rangers jersey; Alicia Ostriker for unrelenting, dazzling poems; Tam-o for hanging in, even after the hand signals; Michael Thomas for tender poems and loving muscle cars; Rupa and Sagan for great days ahead; Donna Greco for opening the sky; RJ Gibson for headspinning poems that wake me up; Sarah Browning for going for it, always; Joy Castro for seeing, for great integrity and killer work; Emily Mohn-Slate, yes! for *The Falls*; Rick Barot for his humanity and original poems; Aiden Angle for going for it; Maria Sticco for good humor and years of amazing work; Michael Waters for his poems of mastery and the New York reading; Maggie Anderson for treasured poems of West Virginia; Michelle Stoner, traveler, for writing it down; Joseph Bathanti, front line man and running back, for deep Pittsburgh; Dr. H. for jokes and cool glasses; Todd Sanders, inventor, for talks on Delaware Ave.; Daniela Buccilli for unrelenting quest; Michael Jones for friendship and opening worlds; Mihaela Moscaliuc for stunning poems that span time and space; Jill West, Queen of the Blues, who sings poetry; Patricia Smith for writing into the heart of it; Marcella Redmund for the hippie story and compassion in Vermillion; Dr. Robin for warm kindness and making sense of the body; all the MFA mentors in Pittsburgh and Ireland, for making the writing real; Sarah Williams-Devereux, poet, teacher, for continuing on the Mad road; Kathy Mangan for loving Pittsburgh; Rachel Walton for exploring without end; Gail Langstroth, the original Mud Fire; Rhoda Mills Sommer, coolest one, for years of invention and patience; Dr. G. for the sea glass; Bobby Marchese, life artist; Pat Bernarding for the Flatiron reading; Lisa Alexander for bringing it up; Liane Ellison Norman for treasured friendship and more mad adventures; Kay Comini for river poems and wild bravery; Lucienne Wald for end rhyme, even in St. Louis; Gerry Rosella Boccella for deep poems of legacy; Tom and Barb for sweet years of friendship; Bounce, cool brother to Don; Michael Wurster, for *Even Then*, poetry hero still; All the Madwomen—for getting madder every year; the Carlow gang—especially Lou, Sigrid, Anne, Roberta, Sarah Williams-Devereux, Tess, for mad support. Matt Gordley, for getting it and bridging worlds; Robert Kracht for loving poems; The Red Dog staff for years of good work and pizza; Britt Horner for loving gardens and books; Brandon Fury for deep Scorpio poems; Colleen K. for making life visible; In memory of: Bob Patak, rock lover who lives in the sky; Dorothy Holley for magic socks and *A Whole Quart Jar*; Jimmy Cvetic, Secret Society of Dog, life-changer who made us all better; Cj Coleman, amazing woman, who wrote the best sex poems; Elicia Parkinson, skywriter and explorer; the spirit of Patricia Dobler that guides us; Peter Oresick for *The Story of Glass* that continues; Anita Gevaudan Byerly for loving trains and *Steam Rising;* Vee for telling it like she saw it; Jay Flory, traveler, for rock 'n' roll paintings; Big Jim Hollowood and the 40 ft. guitar; R. T. Beatty and Charlotte Thoma, who are with me always; to Don, my heart of hearts.

9 780822 966241